AMERICA AT WAR

THE IRAQ WAR

12 THINGS TO KNOW

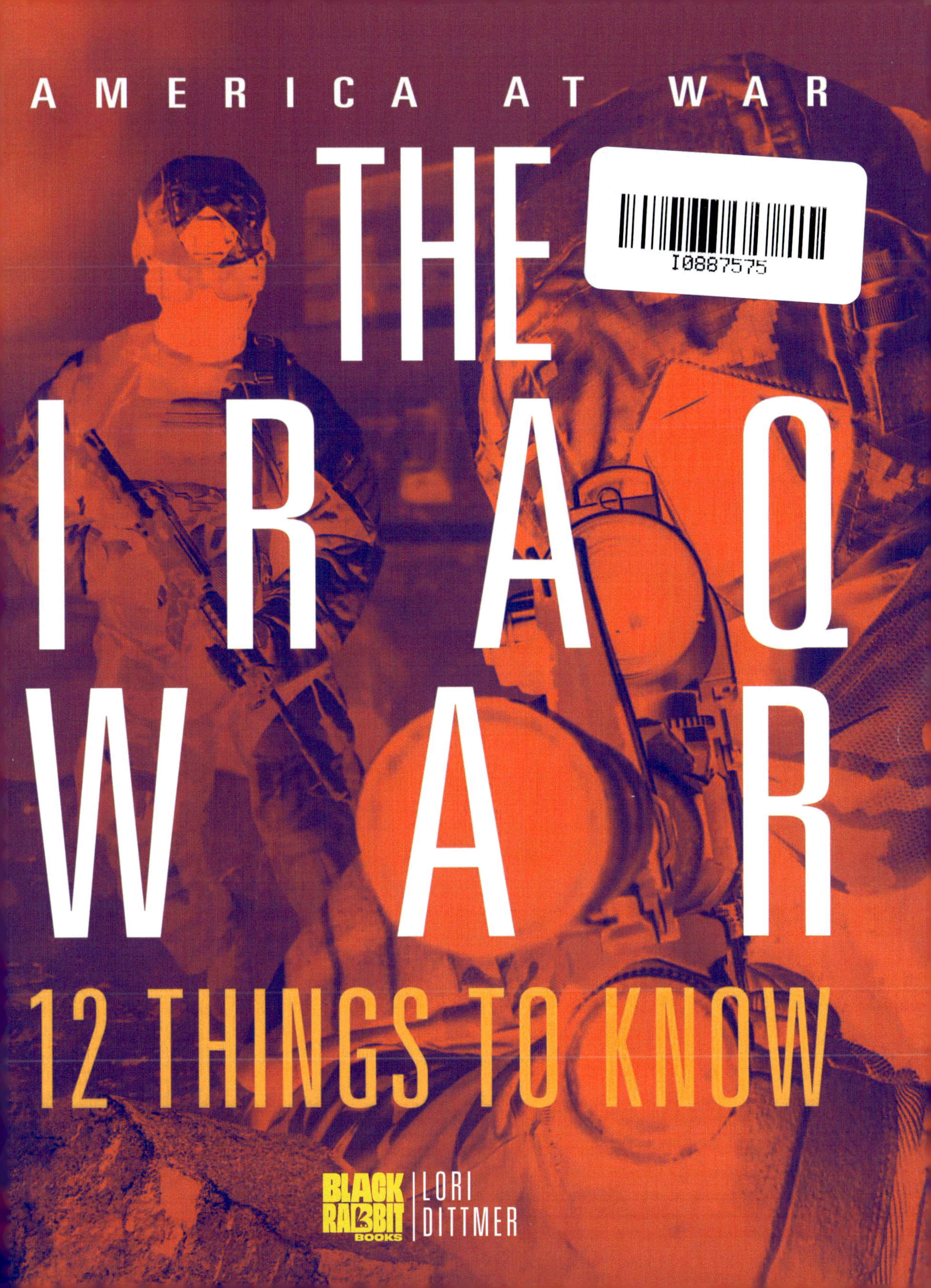

LORI DITTMER

BLACK RABBIT BOOKS

Table of Contents

Ballistic missiles can travel far distances and are seen as a military threat to nearby countries.

Saddam Hussein Invades *Kuwait*

1

In 1988, Iraq ended a war with Iran. To fund the war, Iraq had borrowed money from other countries. Iraq leader Saddam Hussein thought these countries should have protected Iraq for free. He asked them to cancel the loans. The countries ignored him.

Kuwait is a small country next to Iraq. It is next to the Persian Gulf. At the time, it did not have a powerful army. But it was rich in oil. Hussein said that oil that belonged to Iraq. On August 2, Hussein sent troops into Kuwait. In just two days, Iraq took control. Hussein now had Kuwait's oil. He also had a path to the Persian Gulf. It led to the Indian Ocean. This access increased his power in the region.

Suddam Hussein

Other world leaders were watching. On January 17, 1991, the United States and its **allies** launched a new operation. It was called Desert Storm. Missiles flew through the air. They took out weapons factories. Ground forces joined the fight on February 24. Four days later, President George H. W. Bush entered the war.

Hussein pulled his troops from Kuwait. He agreed to get rid of **weapons of mass destruction**. But he did not keep his word. In 1998, the United States and Great Britain sent an **air strike**. It lasted four days. It destroyed places where weapons might be made and stored. But Hussein continued to keep out weapons inspectors.

Iraqi military aircraft

Oil burns in the aftermath of Operation Desert Storm.

700 Number of oil wells set on fire by Iraqi troop as they left Kuwait.

Giant clouds of smoke gave off deadly fumes. • The fires burned for months. • This hurt Kuwait's economy and environment.

September 11 Attacks Shake the *United States*

2

Clear skies turned fiery on the morning of September 11, 2001. At 8:46 a.m., an airplane flew through New York. It hit the North Tower of the World Trade Center. At first, no one knew what had caused the crash. Was it an accident? Had the pilot lost control?

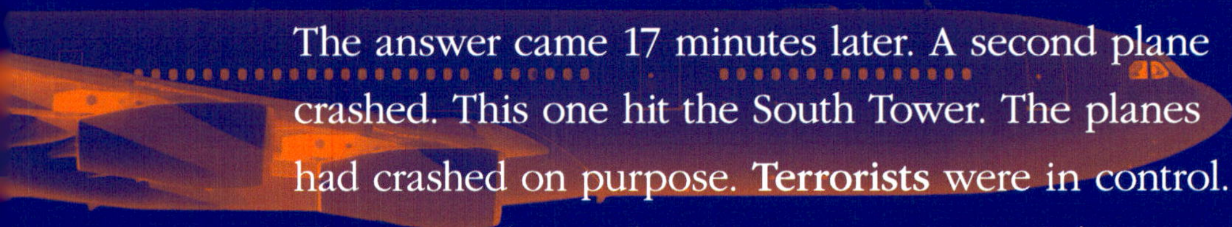

The answer came 17 minutes later. A second plane crashed. This one hit the South Tower. The planes had crashed on purpose. **Terrorists** were in control. They used the airplanes as weapons. By 9:45 a.m., the United States and Canada ordered all planes to land.

Meanwhile, the towers in New York were in trouble. Burning jet fuel leaked from the planes. This weakened the steel beams that held up the buildings. Rescue workers rushed to rescue as many people as possible. Both towers fell within two hours of being hit.

The fire and smoke from the towers lasted months.

19 Number of terrorists combined on all four flights.

It is the deadliest terrorist attack in history. • All US planes were grounded until September 13. • The attacks caused $10 billion in damages.

The towers were not the only targets that day. One plane crashed into the Pentagon in Virginia. This is the base for the US Department of Defense. Another plane was heading to Washington, DC. People on board figured out what was happening. They fought with the terrorists. The plane crashed in a field. It didn't do any other damage.

Nearly 3,000 people died in the four attacks. Later, a group called al-Qaeda claimed responsibility.

REMEMBERING 9/11 Memorial Plaza opened 10 years after the attacks. Two giant reflecting pools now stand in the footprints of the North and South Towers. This area is called Ground Zero. Each pool contains a 30-foot (9.14-meter) waterfall. Bronze walls show the names of those who died. The 9/11 Museum is beneath the Plaza

War on Terror Begins *in Afghanistan*

3

On September 20, 2001, President George W. Bush gave a speech. The War on Terror was about to begin. The main target was the terrorist group al-Qaeda. It followed an extreme form of Islam. Most Muslims rejected its ideas.

Afghanistan was led by a group called the Taliban. They let al-Qaeda operate there. The United States wanted to remove the Taliban from power. This would take support away from al-Qaeda.

The first mission began on October 7, 2001. It was called Operation Enduring Freedom. US forces bombed the country. Ground troops moved in 12 days later. The Taliban fled into the countryside. Some leaders escaped into Pakistan. In February 2002, the United Nations (UN) helped Afghanistan start a new government.

Taliban members were on the run. But they did not give up. UN troops stayed in Afghanistan. They worked to rebuild the country. They trained Afghan security forces. They helped the people stay safe from Taliban attacks. The war dragged on.

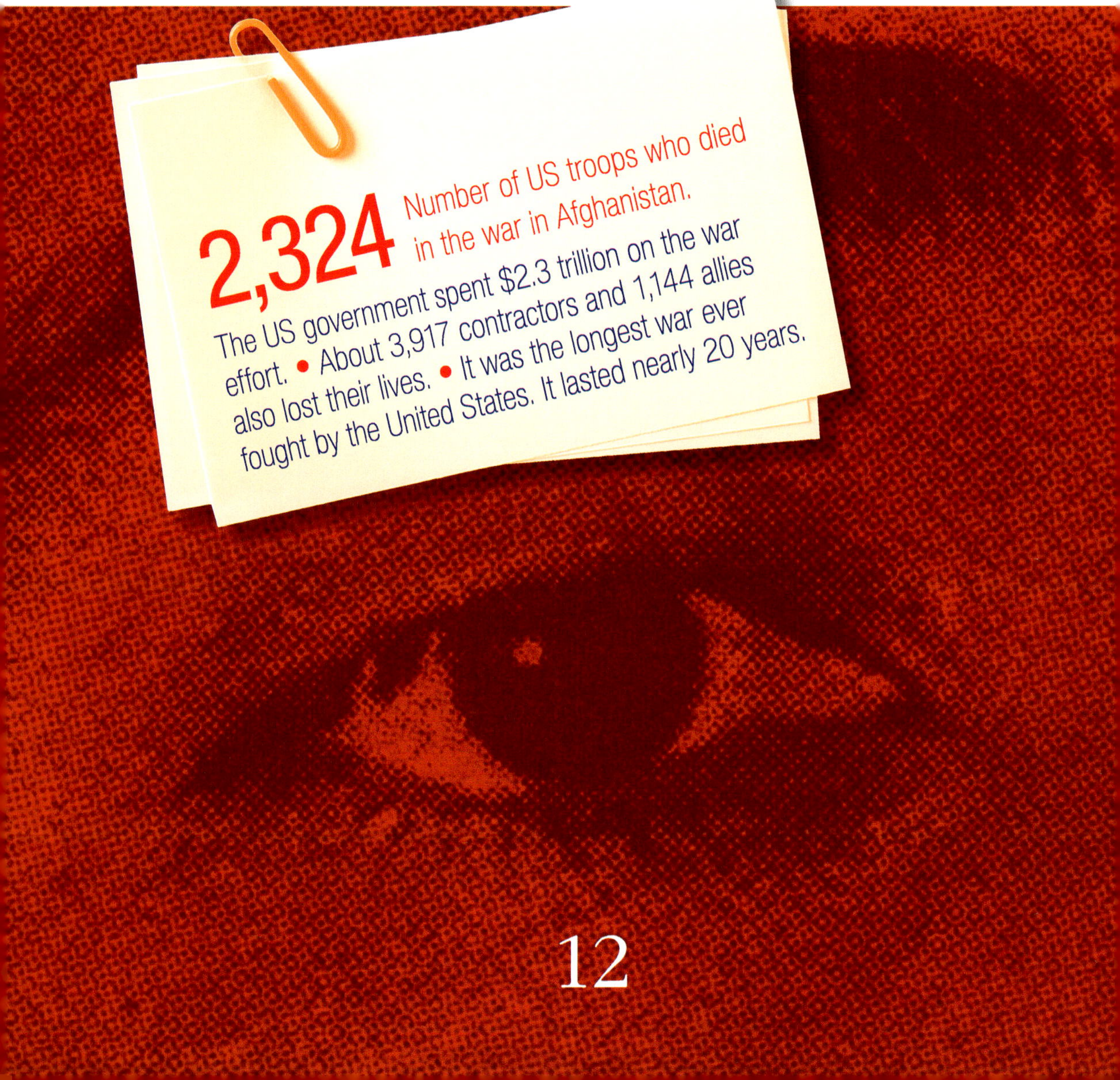

2,324 Number of US troops who died in the war in Afghanistan.

The US government spent $2.3 trillion on the war effort. • About 3,917 contractors and 1,144 allies also lost their lives. • It was the longest war ever fought by the United States. It lasted nearly 20 years.

The mission ended in 2014. About 13,000 troops stayed for support. The rest went home in 2021. But the Taliban came back right after. It took over again. The new government collapsed.

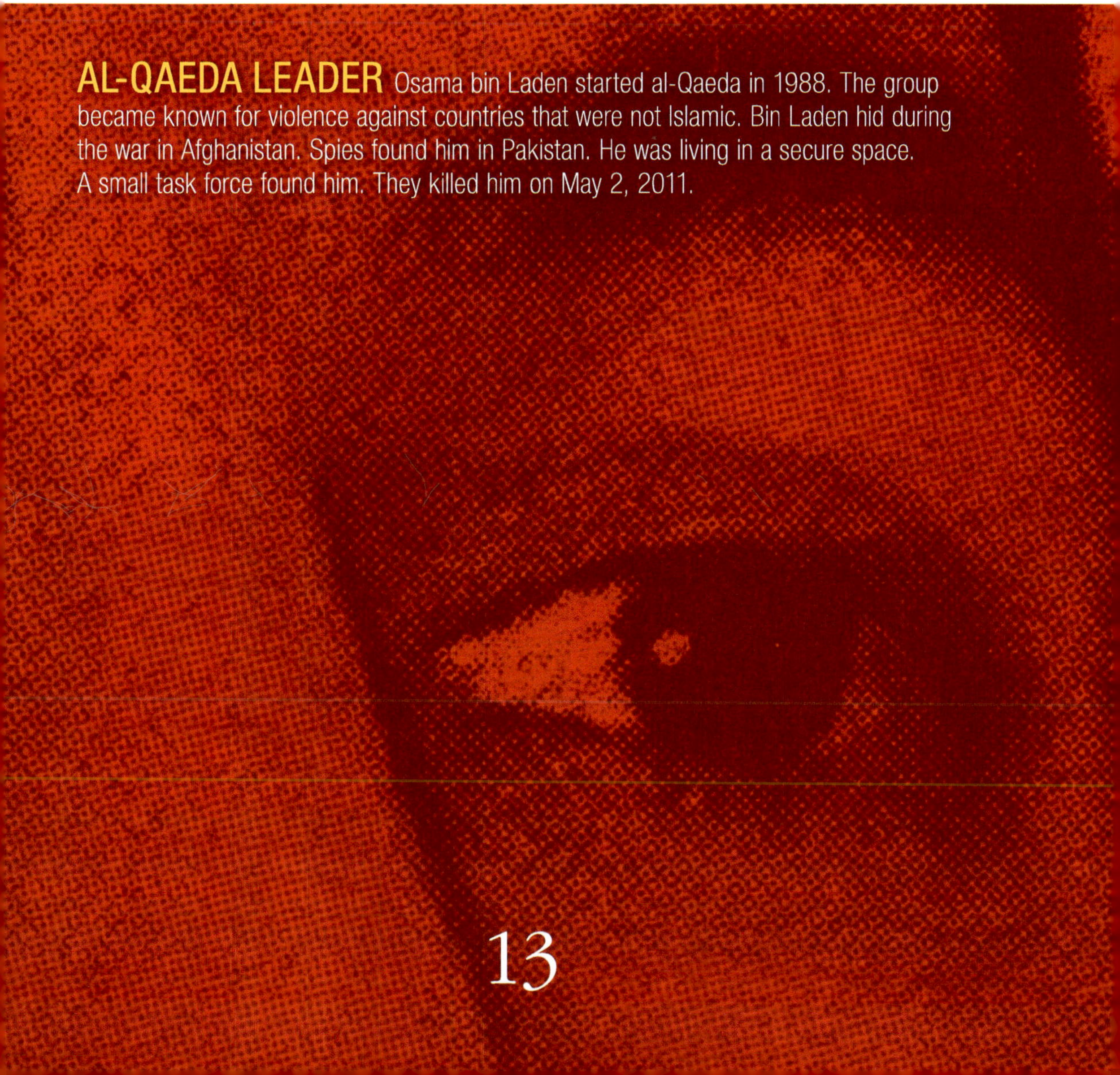

AL-QAEDA LEADER Osama bin Laden started al-Qaeda in 1988. The group became known for violence against countries that were not Islamic. Bin Laden hid during the war in Afghanistan. Spies found him in Pakistan. He was living in a secure space. A small task force found him. They killed him on May 2, 2011.

US-Led Forces Bring Down *Saddam Hussein*

4

By 2002, US troops had sent the Taliban into hiding. A new Afghan government was taking shape. Now, it was time to take care of Iraq. The US government believed Hussein had helped al-Qaeda. They were sure that Iraq had hidden weapons of mass destruction.

On March 17, 2003, President Bush demanded Hussein leave Iraq. He gave Hussein 48 hours. Hussein refused. In the morning of March 20, the US and allied forces took action. They launched Operation Iraqi Freedom. It began with an air strike. Then troops flooded Kuwait in the south. They quickly took control of Baghdad, the capital city.

The combat was over by May 1. The Iraqi government fell. But Hussein and other Iraqi leaders escaped. US troops spent months searching. In December, they found him. He was hiding in a hole in the ground.

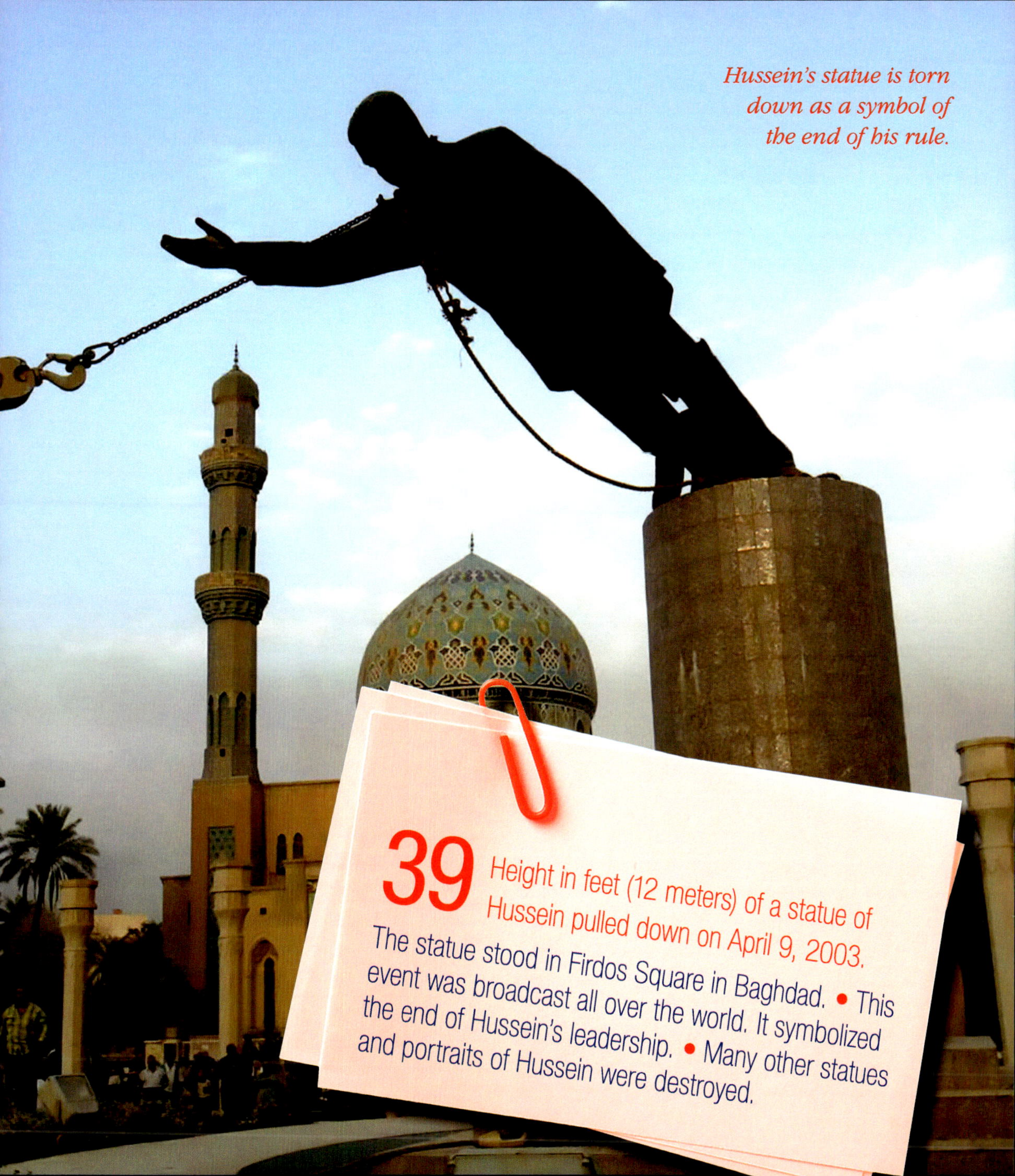

Hussein's statue is torn down as a symbol of the end of his rule.

39 Height in feet (12 meters) of a statue of Hussein pulled down on April 9, 2003.

The statue stood in Firdos Square in Baghdad. • This event was broadcast all over the world. It symbolized the end of Hussein's leadership. • Many other statues and portraits of Hussein were destroyed.

BATTLING THE SANDSTORM Just days after the invasion, a severe sandstorm swept through Iraq. The sky turned red with dust. Rain turned to mud. Weather forecasts helped US troops decide where to go. Planes used satellites to guide the way. The system knew where to drop bombs.

Hussein was put on trial. It lasted nine months. Hussein was found guilty of crimes against humanity. He was sentenced to death. An Iraqi court agreed with this decision. Hussein was **executed** in December 2006. No weapons of mass destruction had been found.

Hussein was arrested on December 14, 2003.

Prisoner Treatment Draws *Backlash*

5

Fighting was meant to stop on May 1, 2003. Still, the war was not over. Rebel fighters pushed back against the US and its allies. US troops tried to stop the attacks. They wanted to protect **civilians**. They also wanted to go home.

To do so, they needed to find Iraqi leaders. The leaders had gone into hiding. Nobody knew where they might be. Some thought prisoners at Abu Ghraib would know. The prison was about 20 miles (32 kilometers) from Baghdad.

Some of the prisoners were terrorists. But many more had done nothing wrong. They had been locked up for no reason. By 2004, photos leaked. They showed the prison conditions. The prisoners were being hurt and humiliated. Some were not allowed to sleep. Others had to wear dog collars. They were frightened by military dogs. They were beaten and chained. Some died.

The images shocked the world. They caused an outrage. The US Army investigated. It found US personnel had taken part in the **abuse**. President Bush apologized for the terrible acts. But the damage was done. One of the United States' goals in Iraq was to free Iraqis from cruelty. Now people questioned if the United States respected the Iraqi people.

In September 2006, the prisoners were moved. Control of Abu Ghraib went back to Iraq.

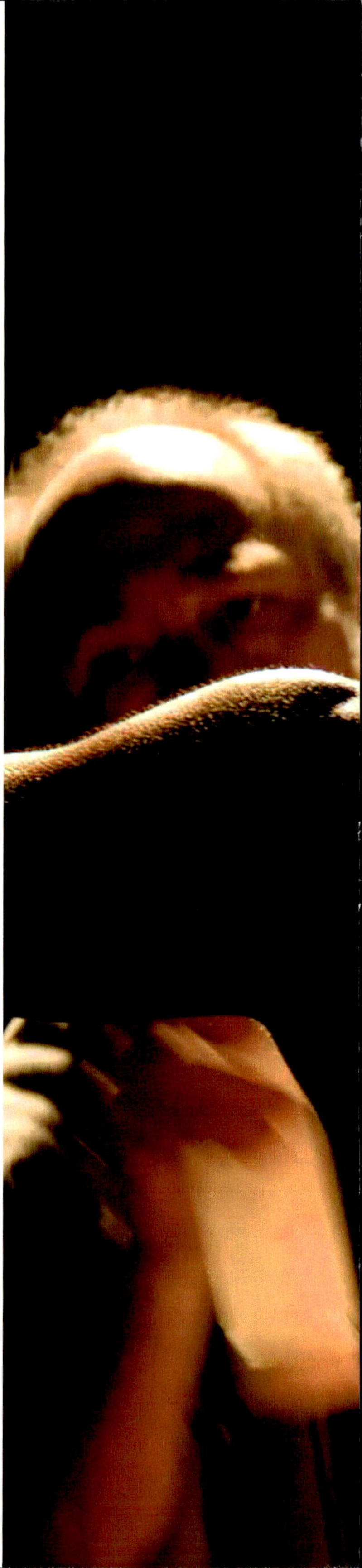

Prisoners were often beaten during interrogations.

11 Number of US soldiers and officers found guilty of crimes against the prisoners.

Many other soldiers were in trouble for their actions. • The prison held almost 4,000 people. • A lawsuit to help the victims went to trial in 2024.

In 2006, prisoners at the Abu Ghraib prison were moved by armed guards.

Bush Redefines Purpose *of Iraq War*

6

After the 9/11 attacks, a **commission** was formed. Its job was to find any security weaknesses before the attacks. They hoped to prevent future attacks. In July 2004, the 9/11 Commission gave a report to the US Congress. It found no proof that Saddam Hussein had worked with al-Qaeda.

In October, the Iraq Survey Group (ISG) sent out a report. The ISG was a group of weapons experts. It looked into weapons of mass destruction in Iraq. It found that the United States did not have proof of these weapons when the war began. Soldiers had found some chemical weapons in Iraq. But they were old and rusted. They had been built before 1991.

Bush shifted the focus of the war. Hussein had been a brutal leader. He had killed anyone who opposed him. Bush said it was good that he was gone. They could now start a **democracy** in Iraq. This was the new purpose of the war.

Violence in Iraq did not stop. More troops died. Many Americans did not like the way Bush handled the war. This became a major issue in the 2004 presidential election. Still, Bush managed to win a second term.

Many Americans thought Bush was a liar and they protested the war.

THINK ABOUT IT

Do you think the United States should have waited to find more proof before invading Iraq? Why or why not?

150 Number of US and allied troops killed between March 30 and May 1, 2003.

By November 2004, that number reached about 1,000. • After the Iraqi government fell, chaos broke out in the country. • The United States tried to help Iraq form a stable new government.

Protesters used thousands of crosses to show the number of Americans killed in the Afghanistan and Iraq wars.

Iraqis Hold First Elections *in 50 Years*

7

During Hussein's rule, Iraqi people had not been allowed to pick their own leaders. On January 30, 2005, they held an election for the new government. It was Iraq's first democratic vote since 1953. American soldiers helped to keep the polling stations safe.

Voters created an assembly of 275 representatives. This group wrote a new **constitution**. They selected Jalal Talabani as president. Talabani then picked Iraq's prime minister. He chose Ibrahim al-Jaafari.

The Sunnis were a **minority** group in Iraq. Many of them did not believe the new government would fix the country's problems. Some refused to vote at all. This meant the Sunnis were not well-represented in politics. They thought this was unfair as well. They tried to change the terms. But they did not get enough

The election was the first time Iraqis could vote in over 50 years.

15,000 Number of US troops who patrolled Baghdad during the January 2005 election.

Voters chose a national assembly of 275 members. • The assembly created a constitution. • Many Sunnis felt they were not well represented.

votes. In December 2005, many Sunnis voted in the general election. This gave them more representatives in the government.

Al-Jaafari was a Shiite. He faced challenges to his leadership. People thought he favored his own group too much. In 2006, he agreed to step down. Another Shiite replaced him. His name was Nouri al-Maliki. Many Sunnis believed he favored his own group too.

Electoral ink is used to stain a person's finger after they vote.

GROUPS IN IRAQ

After the Iraq War, the main groups in the country were Shiites, Sunnis, and Kurds. Shiites were the largest group. The Shiites and Sunnis each follow a different version of Islam. The Kurds have their own language and culture. But they follow either the Sunni and Shiite religion.

New Technologies Keep Soldiers *Safe*

8

Iraq had a new leader. The government was more balanced. But US troops stayed in the country. **Insurgent** groups fought against the changes. These groups made their own weapons. **IEDs** were the biggest threats to troops. These bombs could have gunpowder, fertilizer, or nails.

Some IEDs were small. They could be sent in a package. Bigger bombs could be hidden on the side of the road. These weapons caused burns or hearing damage. Material thrown from the bombs could rip through skin. This led to major bleeding. Many soldiers were wounded or killed by IED attacks.

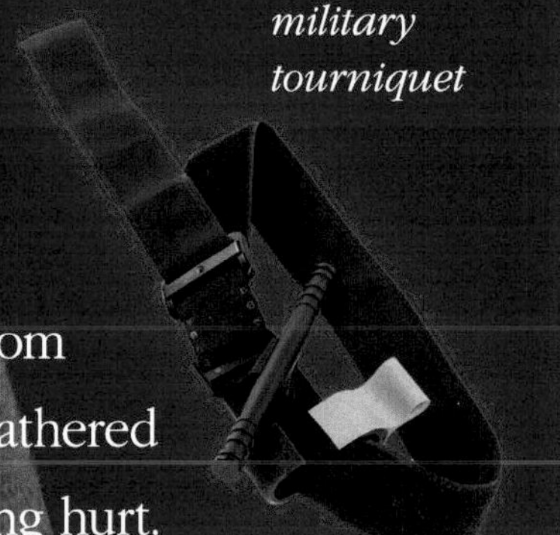

military tourniquet

The US military used drones to stop the bombs from being planted. The drones watched roads. They gathered information safely. Soldiers were not at risk of being hurt. But drones could not see everything. IEDs were still a risk.

MEDICAL IMPROVEMENTS Military doctors found new ways to save lives in Iraq. Many soldiers bled to death from their injuries. They could not get to the hospital in time to be treated. Doctors began improving their use of tourniquets. These devices wrap around an arm or leg to stop bleeding. A new special powder also helped slow bleeding.

$50 billion Amount of money the United States spent on MRAPs in Iraq and Afghanistan.

More than 12,000 MRAPs were sent to these areas. • IEDs were often planted on roadsides or delivered in vehicles. • Drones helped soldiers look for suspicious activity.

Special trucks helped keep troops safe. These were called Mine-Resistant Ambush-Protected (MRAP) Vehicles. They could withstand blasts. Some MRAPs had long robotic arms. The arms could pick up IEDs. Other MRAPs had radio jammers. These blocked signals. This kept some IEDs from exploding.

An army task force heads out on patrol with armed soldiers and trucks.

Fighting Takes a Toll *on Iraqi People*

9

Fighting between Iraqi groups ramped up in 2006. On February 22, members of al-Qaeda in Iraq (AQI) bombed a Shiite holy place. AQI wanted to start a civil war. It worked. Violence broke out between Sunnis and Shiites. US troops and the Iraqi government tried to help. But the violence got worse.

Most Iraqi citizens were not part of the fighting. But their lives were affected. Chaos broke out in their towns and cities. Conditions were dangerous. People were forced to flee their homes. By the start of 2008, 4.7 million Iraqis were **displaced**. Some stayed in the country. Many more left. Nearby Syria and Jordan took them in.

Often, **refugees** were viewed with suspicion. Other countries worried that violence was not far behind.

Refugee camps often have makeshift shelters made out of cloth and plastic tarps.

Many refugees had to walk hundreds of miles (km) to escape Iraq.

THINK ABOUT IT

Imagine your family is forced to leave home and go to a new place. Where would you go? What do you think your life would be like?

Eventually, Jordan made a new law. It would not allow Iraqi men between the ages 18 to 35 to enter its borders. Syria also put limits on those who could enter.

Refugees faced other problems. Many did not have clean water. Disease, such as cholera, spread. Those in new countries had a hard time finding jobs. Living conditions were poor.

60,000 Number of Iraqi citizens who fled their homes each month during 2007.

Two million Iraqis fled to other nations. • Those who fled faced poor treatment and living conditions. • Many of those who tried to return found their homes destroyed.

10 US Troops Surge to Keep *the Peace*

A turning point in the war came in 2007. Fighting raged across Iraq. Citizens questioned whether their government could keep the country together. The United Nations wanted to pull troops out of Iraq. But it feared the Iraqi government would fall without support. If that happened, the Sunnis, Shiites, and terrorist groups would struggle for power.

In January, President Bush announced a new plan. The United States would send more soldiers to Iraq. About 130,000 were already there. Bush and military leaders from other countries planned to partner with Iraqi communities. They wanted to find terrorists and keep peace in neighborhoods. The new plan became known as the Surge.

Later that year, more than 20,000 troops arrived in Iraq. Then groups of Sunnis began to help. They went to work with the US and Iraqi governments. Many had fought

Most of the new troops protected Iraq's capital city, Baghdad.

against the troops. Now, they helped fight terrorists. Violence went down. The government showed signs of progress.

Laws had kept many Sunnis from holding government jobs. In January 2008, the Iraqi government got rid of the laws. Still, the country was unstable. If troops left too quickly, the government could fall apart.

19 Number of US deaths in Iraq in May 2008.

It was the fewest since the start of the war. • Sunni groups began working with the Iraqi government in June 2007. • In January 2008, the Iraqi government allowed Sunnis to work in government jobs.

Special task forces carried out raids and found hidden terrorists during the Surge.

US Forces Slowly Leave *Iraq*

11

For a long time, Sunni insurgents controlled the Anbar Province in Iraq. Terrorist groups operated there. It was a deadly place for US soldiers. Then, Sunnis began helping US troops. The number of attacks dropped. With growing Sunni support, the United States began pulling troops from the region. Other areas in Iraq improved too.

Near the end of his last term, President Bush put a plan in place. The United States would withdraw from Iraq. In November 2008, Barack Obama was elected to be the next US president. By then, the war in Iraq had gone on for five years. Iraq finally appeared stable. The Iraqi government agreed to the timetable. US troops would leave by the end of 2011.

US military duffle bag

By June 30, 2009, most Iraqi cities and towns were already free of military presence. Across the nation, Iraqis celebrated. Still, some tension remained. The Sunnis still wanted more power in the government. Others had doubts about Iraq's military strength. But most Iraqis were pleased.

Some troops stayed in Iraq through 2011. They helped to train Iraqi security forces. In December 2011, the last soldiers left Iraq. The country was working to become a democratic nation. But it still had a long way to go.

VOTING AGAIN Iraqis returned to the polls in 2010. Explosions rattled Baghdad and other cities. But most Iraqis carried on with the vote. More than 60 percent of voters cast their ballots. They elected the most diverse group in the country's history. All the major political and ethnic groups were represented.

4,500 Estimated number of US soldiers who died in the war.

More than 1 million US airmen, soldiers, sailors, and Marines served in Iraq. • The US Department of the Treasury spent $800 billion during the war. • The last US soldiers left Iraq on December 18, 2011.

A man casts his vote in the Iraqi general election in 2010.

12 ISIS Gains Ground in the *Middle East*

Shortly after US troops left Iraq, tensions flared. It began when the government announced it would arrest a Sunni vice president. He was linked to the deaths of Iraqi politicians. Sunnis felt threatened. The move took away their power.

The terrorist group AQI saw a chance to grow its power. It found new members in Sunni areas. Soon AQI joined other extreme groups. They formed the Islamic State (ISIS). ISIS took control of the Anbar Province. In 2014, ISIS captured new territory. This included Iraq's second-largest city, Mosul. The group also moved into neighboring Syria.

Haider al-Abadi became prime minister of Iraq in 2014. He worked to include Sunnis in the government. He called for unity to fight against ISIS. President

Obama said the United States would support the Iraqi government. The United States restarted its mission to help the Iraqi military. About 2,500 US troops went to Iraq. They lived on bases with Iraqi troops.

In July 2017, al-Abadi announced that Iraqi forces had taken back Mosul. Later that year, both Syria and Iraq said that ISIS was defeated. Still, ISIS continues to operate around the world.

ISIS flag

ISIS captured and killed Syrian Army soldiers in March 2018.

95 Percentage of territory ISIS lost by December 2017.

ISIS is also known as Daesh. • Pockets of the group are still active around the Middle East and in Africa. • ISIS continues to be a global threat.

An F-15E fighter jet flies over Syria during a mission to support Operation Inherent Resolve

OPERATION INHERENT RESOLVE After the Iraq War, US troops began a new mission. Operation Inherent Resolve started in 2014. Its focus was to fight ISIS. There are forces from more than 30 countries. US troops lead the attacks. The mission supports Iraqi and Syrian forces. In September 2024, US and Iraqi leaders agreed to wind down the operation.

12 Key Dates

January 17, 1991
The United States begins Operation Desert Storm.

September 11, 2001
Al-Qaeda terrorists hijack four US planes and use them as weapons.

October 7, 2001
The United States begins Operation Enduring Freedom in Afghanistan.

March 19, 2003
The United States turns its focus to the war in Iraq.

April 28, 2004
Photos of prisoner abuse at Abu Ghraib appear on US television.

October 6, 2004
The Iraq Survey Group releases a report saying there are no weapons of mass destruction in Iraq.

January 17, 1991

September 11, 2001

January 30, 2005
Iraqis vote in the country's first free elections in more than 50 years.

October 15, 2005
Iraqis approve the country's new constitution.

February 22, 2006
An AQI attack on Shiite triggers a rise in fighting.

January 12, 2008
The Iraqi government gets rid of laws keeping Sunnis from working in the government.

August 31, 2010
US combat operations end in Iraq.

December 18, 2011
All US troops exit Iraq.

April 28, 2004

January 30, 2005

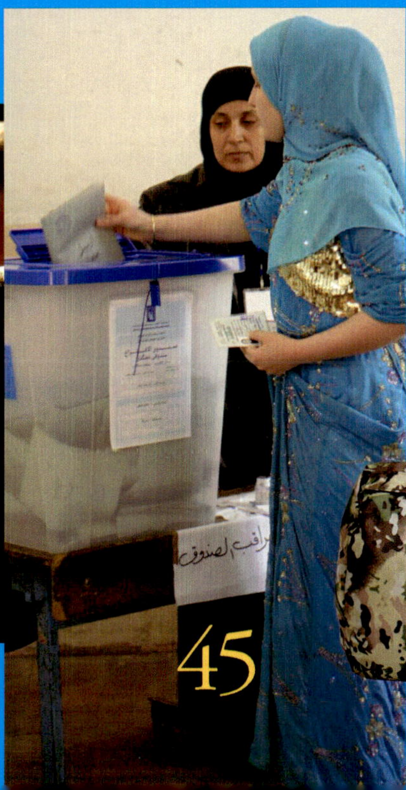

December 18, 2011

Glossary

abuse
Poor treatment of someone or something, either with words or with physical actions.

air strike
An attack in which military planes drop bombs.

ally
A country that supports and helps another country in a war.

civilian
A person not in the armed services.

commission
A group of people given the official job of finding information or controlling something.

constitution
The system of beliefs and laws by which a country, state, or organization is governed.

democracy
A form of government in which people choose leaders by voting.

displace
To force people to leave the area where they live.

executed
Killed as punishment for a crime.

IED
Stands for improvised explosive device; a simple bomb made and used by unofficial or unauthorized forces.

insurgent
A person who fights against the established government.

minority
A number or amount that is less than half of a total.

refugee
A person who is forced to leave a country for safety, usually because of war or for religious reasons.

terrorist
Someone who uses violence to scare people, often to achieve a political goal.

weapon of mass destruction
A nuclear, chemical, or biological weapon that causes widespread death and destruction.

For More Information

Books

Hassig, Susan M. *Iraq*. Buffalo, NY: Cavendish Square Publishing, 2024.

Rebman, Nick. *9/11 Terrorist Attacks*. Mendota Heights, MN: Apex Editions, 2025.

Websites

A Nation Goes to War
education.nationalgeographic.org/resource/a-nation-goes-to-war/

Iraq War
kids.britannica.com/students/article/Iraq-War/574392

Timeline: The Iraq War
www.cfr.org/timeline/iraq-war

About the Author

Lori Dittmer has written more than 80 nonfiction books for children. She is passionate about creating books that inspire curiosity and a love for learning in young readers. She lives with her husband in southern Minnesota. In her free time, she enjoys reading, hiking, and going on adventures with her family.

Index

 • Top Rank is an imprint of Black Rabbit Books. • Designed by Danny Nanos • Photographs © Alamy Stock Photo/Cinematic Collection, 18–19, 44–45, DOD Photo, 16, Handout, 41, US Army Photo, 42–43; Dreamstime/Andrew Chittock, 44, Eriklam, 18, Hikrcn, 31, Karen Foley, 7, Mark Higgins, 21, 23, Nikolay Yeltsov, 28, Prazis, 34, Senohrabek, 2, 8, Sergiy Romanyuk, 32–33; Getty Images/ALI JASIM/AFP, 17, 20; Shutterstock/Andrii__Ivaniuk, 37, 45, anmbph, 27, Belinda Pretorius, 48, breakermaximus, cover, 1, 34–35, CHRIS POOK, 40, Farzad Abdollahi, 6, Georgy Dzyura, 16, Jack_the_sparow, 27, Jacob Lund, 37, Jolygon, 46–47, Joseph Sohm, 22, maradon 333, 4-5, Niyazz, 38, Prachaya Roekdeethaweesab, 5, 12–13, railway fx, 41, Ryanzo W. Perez, 28–29, Sadik Gulec, 24, 25, 45, 39, Steve Allen, 11, Tatohra, 26, Vera Larina, 36, WESTOCK PRODUCTIONS, 30, Whitelion61, 2–3, 9; Wikimedia Commons/Corporal Alicia M. Garcia, U.S. Marine Corps, 14, FaceMePLS, 10, public domain, 15, 26, rds323, 44

Library of Congress Cataloging-in-Publication Data: Names: Dittmer, Lori, author. | Title: The Iraq War: 12 things to know / by Lori Dittmer. | Description: Mankato, MN: Top Rank is an imprint of Black Rabbit Books, [2026] | Series: America at war | Includes bibliographical references and index. | Ages 9–13 | Grades 4–6 | Identifiers: LCCN 2024050095 | ISBN 9781644668221 (library binding) | ISBN 9781644668542 (paperback) | ISBN 9781644668863 (ebook) | Subjects: LCSH: Iraq War, 2003–2011—Miscellanea—Juvenile literature. | Iraq War, 2003–2011—United States—Miscellanea—Juvenile literature | Classification: LCC DS79.763 .D58 2026 | DDC 956.7044/3—dc23/eng/20241129 | LC record available at https://lccn.loc.gov/2024050095